CONTENTS

Introduction

Subjects [Abbreviation]:	First Text:	Page:
1. Bible [Bi]	Luke 24:44	8
2. Deity of Christ [DC]	Genesis 1:26	8
3. Jesus Our Savior [JOS]	Romans 6:23	8
4. Holy Spirit [HS]	Acts 1:8	9
5. Creator [Cr]	John 1:1-3, 14	9
6. Four Kingdoms [FK]	Daniel 2:1	9
7. Ministry of Angels [A]	Psalm 103:20	16
8. Spiritualism [Sp]	Exodus 7:11-13	17
9. Born Again [BA]	Jeremiah 17:9	17
10. Faith and Trust [FT]	Hebrews 11:1, 6	17
11. Walking in the Light [WL]	1 John 1:7-9	17
12. Education [Ed]	Ecclesiastes 12:11, 12	18
13. Prayer [Pr]	Psalm 27:14	18
14. God's People [GP]	Ephesians 4:5	18
15. God's Remnant [GR]	1 Corinthians 1:10	19
16. Witnessing [W]	Luke 22:32	19
17. False Believers [FB]	Daniel 7:25	19
18. Baptism [Bap]	Matthew 28:19	19

19. Foot Washing [FW]	John 13:4-17	20
20. Spiritual Gifts [SG]	1 Thessalonians 5:20	20
21. Ten Commandments [TC]	Titus 2:11	20
22. Sabbath (Seventh Day) [Sab]	James 4:17	21
23. Sabbath observance [SO]	Exodus 20:8-11	21
24. Sunday (First Day) [Sun]	Genesis 1:5	21
25. Mark of the Beast [MB]	Daniel 7:23-25	24
26. Tithing [T]	Deuteronomy 8:18	25
27. Christian Standards [CS]	James 4:4	26
28. Temple of God [TOG]	1 Peter 1:15, 16	26
29. Healing the Sick [HS]	Matthew 4:23	27
30. Marriage [Mar]	Genesis 2:24	27
31. Premarital Sex [PS]	1 Corinthians 7:1, 2, 9	27
32. Second Coming [SC]	Joel 2:31	28
33. Death [De]	Genesis 2:7	28
34. Hell [He]	John 3:16	29
35. 1,000-Year Reign [TYR]	Revelation 20:1-3	29
36. Sanctity of Life [SL]	Psalm 139:13-16	29
37. Judgment [J]	Ecclesiastes 3:17	30
38. Heaven and New Earth [HNE]	1 Corinthians 13:12	30

Summary

Let's Review

Bible Marking
GUIDE

An easy Bible marking system that chain-references texts for 38 Bible topics!

JOHN EARNHARDT

"*As we near the end of time, falsehood will be so mingled with truth that only those who have the guidance of the Holy Spirit will be able to distinguish truth from error. We need to make every effort to keep the way of the Lord. We must in no case turn from His guidance to put our trust in man. . . . Every day we are to come to the Lord with full assurance of faith and to look to Him for wisdom. . . . Those who are guided by the Word of the Lord will discern with certainty between falsehood and truth, between sin and righteousness.*"
—Ellen G. White

To order additional copies of *Bible Marking Guide*, by John Earnhardt, call 1-800-765-6955. Visit us at www.reviewandherald.com for information on other Review and Herald® products

Review and Herald® Publishing Association
Since 1861 / www.reviewandherald.com
Copyright © 2008 by Review and Herald® Publishing Association
Published by Review and Herald® Publishing Association

All rights reserved. No portion of this book may be reproduced, stored in a retrieval system, or transmitted in any form or by any means (electronic, mechanical, photocopy, recording, scanning, other), except for brief quotations in critical reviews or articles, without the prior written permission of the publisher.

The Review and Herald® Publishing Association publishes biblically based materials for spiritual, physical, and mental growth and Christian discipleship.

The author assumes full responsibility for the accuracy of all facts and quotations as cited in this book.

Texts credited to NEB are from *The New English Bible.* ©The Delegates of the Oxford University Press and the Syndics of the Cambridge University Press 1961, 1970. Reprinted by permission.

This book was
Edited by Gerald Wheeler
Copyedited by James Cavil
Cover designed by Trent Truman
Interior designed by Tina M. Ivany
Cover art by Pencil and line: ©iStockphoto.com/helloyiying, Open Bible: ©iStockphoto.com/ze

Typeset: Bembo 11/13

Printed by Pacific Press® Publishing Association
PRINTED IN U.S.A.

Library of Congress Cataloging-in-Publication Data

Earnhardt, John.
  Bible marking guide / John Earnhardt.
    p. cm.
  1. Bible—Reading. I. Title.
  BS617.E27 2008
  220.071—dc22
                   2008039428
  ISBN 978-0-8280-2400-6

January 2020

INTRODUCTION

Bible Marking Guide contains 38 Bible studies and groups of texts. We send it forth with the prayer that it may aid many in becoming better acquainted with the Book of all books—the Bible—thus encouraging them to become faithful and wise representatives of their Lord and Master.

Anyone can give Bible studies by using this easy chain reference method!

HERE'S HOW:
1. On a flyleaf in the front of your Bible, insert a photocopy of the "contents" page of this booklet (pp. 5, 6) that lists all the subjects/abbreviations and first texts.
2. The second step in marking your Bible is to:
    a. Turn to the *first* text for that topic, underline it, and write the *second* text in the margin. Example: In the case of "Jesus Our Savior," turn to Romans 6:23, underline it, and in the margin write: JOS-2 Acts 4:12.
    b. Then, in the margin of Acts 4:12, write the *third* text to study: JOS-3 Isa. 53:6.
3. Follow this same pattern until the last text. In the margin after the last text, write: JOS—End.

Continue with the second subject, and so on, until you have finished chain-referencing all 38 subjects.

HINTS:
- *Always* remember both to have prayer before you study together with others, and at the end of the session.
- It is helpful to underline the key words in each Bible passage that you want to emphasize in your study. Example: Romans 6:23: "For the *wages of sin* is *death;* but the *gift of God* is *eternal life through Jesus Christ* our Lord." Acts 4:12 is the next verse.
- When giving a Bible study, take turns reading the text aloud with the other individual(s) involved. (It will really impress people that you use only the Bible!)

STUDIES IN THIS GUIDE

1. BIBLE [Bi]
The Bible from Genesis to Revelation is still relevant upon God's people today, and God continues to speak to us through His Word.

1—Luke 24:44	7—John 17:17	13—2 Peter 1:20, 21
2—Heb. 4:12	8—Job 23:12	14—Acts 17:11
3—2 Tim. 3:15-17	9—Ps. 119:9, 11	15—John 5:39
4—Rom. 15:4	10—Ps. 119:105	16—Isa. 28:10
5—Jer. 15:16	11—Ps. 119:130	
6—Ps. 12:6, 7	12—Isa. 40:8	

2. DEITY OF CHRIST [DC]
Christ can save us only because He is fully God.

1—Gen. 1:26	6—Micah 5:2	11—Heb. 2:17
2—John 1:1-3, 14	7—John 10:30	12—John 16:27, 28
3—Heb. 1:8	8—Matt. 16:27	13—John 17:4, 5
4—Matt. 3:15-17	9—Col. 2:9	
5—John 17:5	10—Luke 1:35	

3. JESUS OUR SAVIOR [JOS]
Salvation comes by receiving Jesus Christ as Lord and Savior.

1—Rom. 6:23	7—Eph. 2:8, 9	13—Isa. 55:6, 7
2—Acts 4:12	8—1 John 5:11	14—Matt. 6:14, 15
3—Isa. 53:6	9—John 1:12	15—Rev. 3:20
4—2 Cor. 5:21	10—John 3:16	16—1 John 1:7-9
5—1 John 5:13	11—Matt. 1:21	
6—Col. 1:14	12—Ps. 130:7, 8	

4. HOLY SPIRIT [HS]
The Holy Spirit is the source and power of the Christian life.

1—Acts 1:8
2—Acts 2:17
3—Acts 5:32
4—John 14:14-16
5—Luke 11:13
6—John 14:26
7—1 Cor. 2:12, 13
8—Luke 10:17, 19
9—Luke 12:11, 12
10—Acts 2:38
11—Eze. 36:27
12—Eph. 4:30

5. CREATOR [Cr]
Jesus Christ is the creator of all things. He alone could redeem fallen humanity.

1—John 1:1-3, 14
2—Eph. 3:9
3—Heb. 1:1, 2
4—Gen. 1:26
5—1 Cor. 8:6

6. FOUR KINGDOMS [FK]
The vision of Daniel 2 takes human history from **Babylon** (606 B.C.), represented by the head of gold; to **Medo-Persia** (539 B.C.), represented by the chest of silver; to **Greece** (331 B.C.), represented by the thighs of brass; to **Rome** (168 B.C.), represented by the legs of iron; to **Rome divided** (A.D. 476), represented by the feet, partly of iron and partly of clay; down to the **second coming of Jesus** (still future), represented by the Rock cut out of the mountain.

1—Dan. 2:1
2—Dan. 2:28, 29
3—Dan. 2:31
4—Dan. 2:2
5—Dan. 2:9-12
6—Dan. 2:16-19
7—Dan. 2:27, 28
8—Dan. 2:32, 33
9—Dan. 2:37, 38
10—Dan. 2:39-45

HEAD—GOLD
BABYLON: 606-539 B.C.

CHEST—SILVER
MEDO-PERSIA: 539-331 B.C.

THIGH—BRASS
GREECE: 331-168 B.C.

LEGS—IRON
ROME: 168 B.C.- A.D. 476

FEET—IRON MIXED WITH CLAY
SHATTERED ROMAN
EMPIRE: A.D. 476-Second Advent

ADDITIONAL NOTES

The prophecy of Daniel 2 spans the centuries from the prophet's day to the return of Jesus Christ. Many regard it as the most remarkable prophecy in the Bible because it is the most comprehensive and was the first to give a consecutive history of the world from Daniel's time to the end.

In Daniel 7 God gave the prophet a vision that also revealed events that would take place all the way to our day. God pictures under appropriate symbols the rise and fall of nations from Daniel's day to the rise of the antichrist. Anyone seeking Bible truth should be concerned about the work of this agency elsewhere symbolized by the deadly number 666 (Rev. 13:18). Every human being sooner or later must choose for or against what Scripture describes as the little-horn power.

In vision Daniel saw four great beasts emerging from the sea, each differing from the other. The fourth beast had 10 horns. Afterward, a little horn sprang up among the 10 and subdued three of them. Clearly the four beasts represent the same four kingdoms described in Daniel 2, a fact confirmed by Daniel 7:23: "The fourth beast shall be the fourth kingdom."

Daniel 7:4—The lion (Babylon) had eagle's wings, denoting the rapidity with which Babylon extended its domain under Nebuchadnezzar.

Daniel 7:5—The bear (Medo-Persia) had three ribs in its mouth, which signify Babylon, Lydia, and Egypt, kingdoms subdued by this power.

Daniel 7:6—The leopard (Greece) had double wings, denoting the extreme swiftness of its conquests. The creature also had four heads, representing the division of Alexander the Great's kingdom among his four generals: Cassander, Lysimachus, Ptolemy, and Seleucus.

Daniel 7:7—The great terrible beast (Rome) had 10 horns, echoing the shattering of the image of Daniel 2.

Little-Horn Power. Daniel next saw something happen that startled him. He witnessed the emergence of "a little-horn power" that had eyes like a human being and a mouth that spoke boastful things. This entity uprooted three other horns. According to history, the armies of Rome destroyed the power of the Heruli in A.D. 493, the Vandals in A.D. 534, and the Ostrogoths in A.D. 538. As we study Daniel 7 we find a number of clues to the identity of the little horn power.

1. Comes into existence among the 10 horns (verse 8). Thus it must be within the territory of the destroyed Roman Empire.
2. Makes its appearance after A.D. 476, since an invading Germanic tribe overthrew the last Roman emperor in A.D. 476 and the united Empire ceased to exist (verse 8). The little-horn power would combine both religious and civil authority.
3. Uproots three—destroys three of the 10 horns. A horn in Scripture depicts powers or kingdoms (verse 8). The Bible often associates the number 10 with the division of something complete in itself into lesser and incomplete units (Lev. 27:30; Deut. 4:13, 14; Matt. 25:1; Luke 19:13, 17; Rev. 17:12). No human kingdom would ever again be as complete as those of the four kingdoms in the vision of Daniel 2.
4. Eyes like eyes of a man (verse 8). Scripture sometimes uses eyes to stand for intelligence or pride. Haughtiness is probably what the symbol intends to depict here. The vision contrasts the being with the eyes and mouth of a man with the being like a son of man of verse 13. The one like a son of man is the Messiah—Christ—and thus the one with the eyes and mouth of a man is a counterfeit or antichrist. The little horn speaks blasphemies, which means this power seeks to take the place of God Himself and claims divine prerogatives (verse 25). We have here counterfeit claims of divinity.
5. Persecutor, for it makes war with God's people (verse 21).
6. Attempts to change God's law (verse 25).
7. Rules for 1,260 years (verse 25).

The Little Horn Identified. *Who is this antichrist power symbolized in the book of Revelation by the number 666?* The president of the United States or some other political leader? A supercomputer? The United Nations? International terrorists? None of these fit the biblical description.

Only one power in all of history can fit all identifying marks. Who is it and can it be proved? The religious administrative system known as the Papacy alone matches the biblical identifying marks. Let's prove it!

1. The Papacy emerged among the shattered divisions of the Roman Empire.
2. The emperor Justinian of the surviving Eastern Roman Empire appointed a pope in A.D. 538 (after A.D. 476) as a political authority as well as religious leader.
3. The Papacy destroyed the Heruli, Vandals, and Ostrogoth tribes be-

cause they opposed the teaching and claims of the papal hierarchy.

4. The Catholic book *Instructions for Non-Catholics* on page 181 says: "The pope is the supreme visible head of the whole church, and that he teaches infallibly what we must believe and do to be saved." Only God can claim infallibility, and for any human being or institution to do so is to place the person or institution on a level with Him. The papal power speaks blasphemies by claiming for itself a divine role. Scripture defines blasphemy as taking upon oneself divine prerogatives or characteristics, as we see when Christ's opponents accused Him of it: "because that thou, being a man, makest thyself God" (John 10:33). Elsewhere the Pharisees charged Jesus with blasphemy in Luke 5:21, because He claimed power to forgive sins, something that only God possesses. But Jesus has such a right because He is the Savior of the world.

Notice what a Catholic Church spokesperson says about the pope: "The pope is of so great dignity and so exalted that he is not a mere man, but as it were God, and the vicar of God."

"The pope is as it were God on earth, sole sovereign of the faithful of Christ, chief of kings, having plentitude of power, to whom has been intrusted by the omnipotent God direction not only of the earthly but also of the heavenly kingdom" (translated from Lucius Ferraris, "Papa, Article II," *Prompta Bibliotheca,* Vol. VI, pp. 25-29).

"We ... hold upon this earth the place of God Almighty" (Pope Leo XIII,. *The Reunion of Christendom,* encyclical letter of Leo XIII, p. 304).

"The pope is not only the representative of Jesus Christ, but he is Jesus Christ Himself hidden under the veil of the flesh" (*The Catholic National,* July 1895).

The Bible teaches that God is the one who forgives our sins because of what Jesus did at Calvary. Catholics teach just the opposite: "A priest does not have to ask God to forgive your sins. The priest himself has the power to do so in Christ's name. Your sins are forgiven by the priest just the same as if you knelt before Jesus Christ and told them to Christ Himself" (*Instructions for Non-Catholics,* p. 93).

Paul describes the coming man of lawlessness (another way of depicting the antichrist) as one "who opposeth and exalteth himself above all that is called God, or that is worshipped; so that he as God sitteth in the temple of God, shewing himself that he is God" (2 Thess. 2:4).

5. In the year A.D. 1208 Pope Innocent III proclaimed a crusade against the Waldenses and Albigenses, fellow Christians who dared to disagree

with certain teachings of the medieval church. Thousands perished. Some have estimated that perhaps millions died as martyrs at the hands of church agents during the Middle Ages.
6. The Papacy freely admits its responsibility for certain changes in Christian teaching. "Thus the church makes many laws that are not found in the Bible. For example, ... it enforces the laws of Sunday worship with the penalty of serious sin" (*Instructions for Non-Catholics*, p. 61).

"The Catholic Church for over one thousand years before the existence of a Protestant, by virtue of her divine mission, changed the day from Saturday to Sunday" (*Catholic Mirror*, September 1893).

7. The Papacy ruled or dominated much of Christianity for 1,260 years. How do we know the time was 1,260 years? According to biblical reckoning, a time is one year, times (the Hebrew word translated "times" literally means "two") is two years, and the dividing of a time is half a year. The rule given in the Bible is that when it uses a day symbolically, it stands for a year (Eze. 4:6; Num. 14:34). Careful study of biblical time prophecy reveals that it is based on a symbolic year of 360 days. (The actual Jewish calendar had a year of 12 lunar months of 28 and 29 days, totaling 354 days, with an extra, or double, twelfth month, added to keep it in sync with the seasons and astronomical movements.) Thus three prophetic years and a half contained 1,260 days, which would be 1,260 years for the continuation of the supremacy of the little horn. The papal supremacy began in A.D. 538, when the Ostrogoths, the last of the three political powers resisting the influence of the Papacy, succumbed. Adding 1,260 years to 538, we come to 1798. And it was in February of that year that a French army under the leadership of General Berthier entered Rome and took the pope prisoner. Revelation 13:3 says that the symbolic beast would receive a deadly wound, and it happened in 1798. The same verse declares: "and his deadly wound was healed: and all the world wondered after the beast." Students of prophecy regard this prophecy as fulfilled in 1929 when Mussolini restored the pope to the Vatican and once more he became a secular ruler, reigning over Vatican City. Today all the world listens to the pope on religious issues—not always following, but listening.

The Great Reformers. Some may say that all this is hard to accept. Don't get me wrong—this prophecy is not speaking against individuals, for the Catholic Church is filled with fine people who love the Lord. Rather, the Bible speaks against any power or system that goes against or contrary to the Word of God. Martin Luther, the founder of the Lutheran Church, never felt free to break with the leadership of the medieval church and some of its teachings until he recognized the papal system as embodying the principles of the antichrist. John Knox's sermon that launched him on his mission as church reformer focused on prophecies that he saw as describing the papal system. John Rogers preached against the papal system, and it resulted in his becoming the first Protestant martyr under the reign of the British queen Mary. Rogers died at the stake at Smithfield, in London. John Huss decried the moral laxity of the clergy, denied Peter as the church's foundation, and declared the Word of God to be the only rule of faith. The Council of Constance convicted him, and he died at the stake. All the reformers were unanimous in the matter. They saw the papal system as reflecting the principles of the antichrist.

Protest. What has happened to the Protestant churches? The word "Protestant" came from a Middle French word that meant "to witness for" or "to stand up" for something. It later came to be used in the sense of witnessing against something or to stand up in opposition to another thing. One who "protested" defended something against another position. Protestants "stood up for" or "witnessed for" the Word of God. Unfortunately, many Protestants have begun to abandon their witness for the Word of God and are joining hands with those who follow the principles of the antichrist power. For the various churches to unite under such principles is a sign of the end, and God says in Revelation 18:4: "Come out of her, my people."

One thing that most denominations have in common and that makes it easier for them to join with each other is a shared belief in Sunday sacredness. Notice what the Catholic Church says about the Sabbath:

"Of course the Catholic Church claims that the change [Saturday Sabbath to Sunday] was her act.... And the act is a mark of her ecclesiastical authority in religious things (H. F. Thomas, chancellor of Cardinal Gibbons).

"The observance of Sunday by the Protestants is an homage they pay, in spite of themselves, to the authority of the [Catholic] church" (*Plain Talk about the Protestantism of Today,* p. 213).

"The Bible says, 'Remember the Sabbath day to keep it holy.' The Catholic Church says, No. By my divine power I abolish the Sabbath day and command you to keep holy the first day of the week.' And lo! The entire civilized world bows down in a reverent obedience to the command of the holy Catholic Church" (Father T. Enright, former president of the Redemptoral College, Kansas City, Missouri).

"Sunday is a Catholic institution, and its claims to observance can be defended only on Catholic principles.... From beginning to end of Scripture there is not a single passage that warrants the transfer of weekly public worship from the last day of the week to the first" (*Catholic Press* [Sydney, Australia], August 1900).

"We observe Sunday instead of Saturday because the Catholic Church, in the Council of Laodicea ... transferred the solemnity from Saturday to Sunday" (*The Convert's Catechism of Catholic Doctrine*, p. 50).

FOUR FACTS NOW STAND OUT IN BOLD RELIEF:
1. The change from Sabbath to Sunday cannot be found in the Bible (see study 22).
2. God predicted that a power in opposition to Him would "think to change" His times and laws.
3. The Papacy openly declares that it has changed God's law.
4. Thus in effect the Papacy exalts itself above God, as forecast by the apostle Paul in 2 Thessalonians 2:3, 4.

God says: "Remember the sabbath day, to keep it holy.... The seventh day is the Sabbath of the Lord thy God" (Ex. 20:8-11).

"And hallow my sabbaths; and they shall be a sign between me and you, that ye may know that I am the Lord your God" (Eze. 20:20).

The Bible says all the world will wonder after the antichrist power (Rev. 13:8).

7. MINISTRY OF ANGELS [A]
Unseen angels always accompany God's followers. They protect His people as they walk in the path of obedience and duty.

1—Ps. 103:20	6—Acts 1:9-11	11—Rev. 5:11
2—Ps. 34:7	7—Heb. 13:2	12—Ps. 68:17
3—Acts 8:26	8—Matt. 13:39	13—Heb. 12:22
4—Heb. 1:13, 14	9—Matt. 24:30, 31	14—Gen. 28:12
5—Matt. 18:10	10—Matt. 25:31	15—Luke 15:10

8. SPIRITUALISM [Sp]
One of Satan's most effective ways to deceive humanity is through counterfeit supernatural manifestations.

1—Ex. 7:11-13
2—Lev. 19:31
3—Lev. 20:6, 27
4—Deut. 18:10-12
5—1 Chron. 10:13
6—Isa. 8:19, 20
7—Rev. 16:13-15
8—2 Cor. 11:13-15
9—1 Tim. 4:1

9. BORN AGAIN [BA]
A person must be spiritually born again, thus changing from his or her old ways and living a clean life reflecting the principles and teachings of Christ. Such an experience comes only through the working of the Holy Spirit upon the heart.

1—Jer. 17:9
2—John 3:3, 5
3—Matt. 18:3
4—Acts 3:19
5—John 3:8
6—Rom. 8:6
7—Ps. 51:10-12
8—Rom. 6:6
9—2 Cor. 5:17
10—Col. 3:1

10. FAITH AND TRUST [FT]
Our salvation totally rests on our trust and total dependence upon God.

1—Heb. 11:1, 6
2—Rom. 5:1
3—James 2:18-26
4—Rom. 10:17
5—1 John 5:4
6—1 Peter 5:7
7—Heb. 12:2
8—Eph. 6:16
9—1 Peter 1:18, 19
10—Prov. 29:25
11—Ps. 91:9-11
12—Ps. 37:3
13—Rev. 21:8
14—Mark 11:22-24
15—Mark 16:16-18

11. WALKING IN THE LIGHT [WL]
Those who have accepted Jesus as their Savior will live according to His teachings.

1—1 John 1:7-9
2—John 12:35, 36
3—John 8:12
4—Col. 2:6
5—Ps. 119:105
6—Ps. 119:130
7—Prov. 4:18
8—John 3:19, 21
9—John 8:31, 32
10—John 12:46
11—John 10:16, 27
12—Prov. 6:23

12. EDUCATION [Ed]
Dedicated Christians will continue to learn throughout their lives on earth.

1—Eccl. 12:11, 12
2—1 Cor. 2:12, 13
3—2 Cor. 11:6
4—1 Peter 4:11
5—Gal. 1:1
6—2 Cor. 10:5

13. PRAYER [Pr]
Through prayer we can talk with God as to a friend.

1—Ps. 27:14
2—Ps. 4:3
3—Matt. 6:6
4—Phil. 4:6
5—1 Thess. 5:17
6—Ps. 55:17
7—John 14:14
8—Mark 11:24, 25
9—Matt. 5:44
10—Matt. 7:7, 8
11—James 1:5-7
12—Matt. 14:23
13—Rom. 8:26
14—1 Peter 4:7
15—Ps. 66:18
16—Prov. 28:9

14. GOD'S PEOPLE [GP]
God's people will obey the Ten Commandments, including the seventh-day Sabbath. They will carry the last message to the world as found in Revelation 14.

1—Eph. 4:5
2—Rev. 12:17
3—Heb. 12:5, 6
4—Isa. 43:10
5—Eph. 5:8
6—John 8:31, 32
7—2 John 9
8—Heb. 8:10
9—Isa. 8:20, 16
10—Eze. 44:23, 24
11—Titus 2:14
12—Jer. 11:4
13—Ex. 19:5
14—Deut. 26:18, 19
15—1 Peter 2:9
16—Eze. 3:17
17—Rev. 18:4
18—James 1:27
19—1 Cor. 1:10
20—Rev. 14:6-12
21—Heb. 4:4-10

15. GOD'S REMNANT [GR]
In the last days before Christ's second coming God has called a people for the task of witnessing in a special way for Him.

1—1 Cor. 1:10	5—1 John 3:6, 8	9—Rom. 9:27, 28
2—Heb. 13:17	6—Zech. 2:7	10—Zeph. 3:12, 13
3—1 Cor. 5	7—Rom. 11:1, 5	11—Rev. 7:3, 4
4—Eph. 5:25-27	8—Joel 2:32	12—Rev. 14:1-3

16. WITNESSING [W]
Every born-again Christian will seek to lead others to Jesus.

1—Luke 22:32	8—Matt. 9:37, 38	15—Matt. 19:29
2—Matt. 28:19, 20	9—Ps. 126:5, 6	16—2 Tim. 2:12
3—Mark 8:38	10—2 Cor. 9:6	17—John 15:20
4—Amos 6:1	11—James 5:20	18—Luke 17:10
5—1 Cor. 9:16, 17	12—2 Tim. 4:2	19—Acts 5:39
6—Rev. 3:15, 16	13—1 Peter 3:15	20—John 14:12
7—Joel 3:14	14—John 15:5	

17. FALSE BELIEVERS [FB]
Apostate Christians preach against the Ten Commandments and will not honor the true Sabbath of God.

1—Dan. 7:25	5—Rev. 12:17	9—Eze. 22:26
2—Rev. 13:13, 14	6—2 Tim. 4:3, 4	10—Isa. 30:9, 10
3—Rev. 13:7, 8	7—2 Tim. 3:5, 7	11—Mal. 2:7-9
4—Rev. 13:16, 17	8—Isa. 9:16	12—1 John 2:3, 4

18. BAPTISM [Bap]
Baptism acknowledges that we are letting God wash our sins away and allowing Jesus to dwell in us. We become a member of His church by baptism.

1—Matt. 28:19	6—Acts 10:47, 48	11—Col. 3:15
2—Mark 16:15, 16	7—Acts 22:16	12—Col. 1:18
3—Acts 2:38	8—Acts 8:38	13—1 Cor. 12:13, 27
4—Acts 8:12	9—Matt. 3:13, 16	
5—Acts 16:31, 33	10—Gal. 3:27	

19. FOOT WASHING [FW]
The ordinance of foot washing is a mark of those who truly follow Jesus.

1—John 13:4-17
2—1 Cor. 10:21
3—1 Cor. 11:24-29
4—John 6:54-58
5—Matt. 26:26-30

20. SPIRITUAL GIFTS [SG]
The continuing gift of prophecy is one of the marks of God's last-day church.

1—1 Thess. 5:20
2—Eze. 13:3
3—Amos 3:7
4—Eze. 44:23, 24
5—Isa. 8:20
6—Jer. 25:4, 5
7—Ps. 19:7, 11
8—Rev. 12:17
9—Rev. 19:10
10—Judges 4:4
11—Luke 2:36
12—Acts 21:9
13—1 John 4:1
14—1 Cor. 12:28
15—Eph. 4:11-13
16—Hosea 12:13
17—2 Kings 17:15, 18
18—2 Chron. 36:15, 16

ADDITIONAL NOTE

First Corinthians 12:1-28 says that the church is to come behind in no gift, and the continuing presence of the gift of prophecy is to be one of the identifying marks of the remnant church. Writings that result from the manifestation of that gift are not to take the place of the Bible itself, but to lead people to a greater study of God's Word.

21. TEN COMMANDMENTS [TC]
Old Testament people were saved by grace, just as God's people are today. The Ten Commandments are binding today, and all who love God will obey them.

1—Titus 2:11
2—Gen. 6:8
3—Ex. 33:12
4—Prov. 3:34
5—Rom. 5:20
6—Rom. 6:14, 15
7—Rom. 3:20
8—1 John 2:3, 4
9—Ex. 31:18
10—Heb. 8:10
11—John 15:10
12—Luke 16:17
13—Matt. 7:21
14—1 John 5:3
15—Prov. 3:1-4
16—Rev. 22:14
17—Rev. 14:12
18—Matt. 19:17
19—Acts 5:29
20—1 John 3:22
21—Ps. 111:7, 8
22—1 John 3:4
23—James 2:10, 12
24—Eccl. 12:13

22. SABBATH (SEVENTH DAY) [Sab]
The fourth commandment speaks about the Sabbath, which is the seventh day of the week. All people under grace will keep the Sabbath. The Sabbath becomes a joy when we know Jesus.

1—James 4:17	7—1 Chron. 17:27	13—Matt. 24:20
2—1 Peter 2:21	8—Lev. 26:2	14—Acts 18:4
3—Luke 4:16	9—Mark 6:2	15—Acts 13:42, 44
4—Matt. 12:8	10—Acts 17:2	16—Isa. 56:1-6
5—Mark 2:27, 28	11—Eze. 20:12	17—Heb. 4:1-11
6—Ex. 20:11	12—Isa. 66:22, 23	

23. SABBATH OBSERVANCE [SO]
The Sabbath is to be kept from Friday sunset to Saturday sunset. The true born-again Christian will find joy and communion with God through honoring the Lord's holy day.

1—Ex. 20:8-11	5—Ex. 16:23	9—Lev. 23:32
2—Ex. 34:21	6—Heb. 10:25	10—Ps. 16:11
3—Lev. 23:3	7—Matt. 12:12	
4—Neh. 13:15-22	8—Isa. 58:13, 14	

24. SUNDAY (FIRST DAY) [Sun]
Only nine texts in the entire Bible mention the first day of the week, and none of them make Sunday a sacred day.

1—Gen. 1:5	4—Mark 16:9	7—John 20:19
2—Matt. 28:1	5—Luke 24:1	8—1 Cor. 16:1, 2
3—Mark 16:1, 2	6—John 20:1	9—Acts 20:7

ADDITIONAL NOTES

SOME POINTS TO CONSIDER:

Q: Which day is the true seventh-day Sabbath?

A: The fourth commandment calls upon God's people to observe the seventh day of the week (Saturday). Those who are saved by grace will delight to keep the Sabbath along with the other commandments. "And when the sabbath was past, Mary Magdalene, and Mary the mother of James, and Salome" "very early in the morning, on the first day of the week ... came unto the sepulchre at the rising of the sun.... And entering into the sepulchre, they saw a young man ... And he saith unto them, Be not affrighted: Ye seek Jesus of Nazareth, which was crucified: he is risen" (Mark 16:1-6). (Note: Everybody knows that Sunday was the Resurrection day. The Sabbath was past when it dawned. Thus it is evident that the Sabbath is Saturday, the day before Sunday.)

Q: But hasn't time been lost and the days of the week changed since the time of Christ?

A: No! Reliable encyclopedias and reference books make it clear that our seventh day is the same one that Jesus kept holy. It is a simple matter of checking.

Q: But isn't the Sabbath for the Jews only?

A: No. Jesus said, "The sabbath was made for man" (Mark 2:27). Thus it is not for the Jews only, but for all humanity everywhere. The Jews did not even exist as a nation until long after God established the Sabbath.

Q: Isn't Acts 20:7-12 proof that the disciples observed Sunday as a holy day?

A: According to the Bible, each day begins at sundown and ends at the next sundown (see Gen. 1:5, 8, 13, 19, 23, 31; Mark 1:32), and the dark part of the day comes first. So Sabbath begins at Friday night sundown and ends Saturday night at sundown. The meeting of Acts 20 took place during the dark part of the first day of the week, what we now call Saturday night. (*The New English Bible* translates the passage as follows: "On the Saturday night in our assembly ... ") It was a Saturday night meeting, and lasted till midnight. Paul was on a farewell tour and knew that he would not see these people again before his death (verse 25). No wonder he preached so long! (No regular weekly service would have lasted all night.) Again, remember that the meeting convened during the dark part of the first day of the week (or what we now call Saturday night), because Paul was "ready to depart on the morrow" (verse 7). The breaking of bread has no holy day significance whatever, because the early Christians broke bread daily (Acts 2:46). We find not the slightest indication in this Scripture passage that the first day is holy, or that these early Christians considered it so. Neither does it offer the remotest evidence that the Sabbath has been changed. The Bible refers to the Sabbath days (including Sunday) as "working days" in Ezekiel 46:1. God has never asked anyone to observe Sunday as a holy day for any reason whatever. Incidentally, Scripture apparently mentions the Acts 20 meeting only because of the miracle of raising back to life the boy who fell out the window.

Q: Doesn't 1 Corinthians 16:1, 2 speak of Sunday school offerings?

A: No, the passage does not refer to a public meeting. Paul asks his readers to set the money aside privately at home. A famine had ravaged Judea (Rom. 15:26; Acts 11:26-30), and Paul was writing to ask the churches in Asia Minor to help the people suffering there. These Christians all kept Sabbath holy, so Paul suggested that on Sunday morning (perhaps the time they paid bills and settled accounts), after the Sabbath was over, they should put aside something for their needy fellow believers so that it would be on hand when he came. It was to be done privately, as the Spanish translation says: "at home." Notice also that the passage does not describe Sunday as a holy day. In fact, the Bible never suggests or commands Sundaykeeping.

Q: But isn't John 20:19 the record of the disciples instituting Sunday-keeping in honor of the Resurrection?

A: On the contrary, the disciples did not yet believe that the Resurrection had taken place (Mark 16:14). They had met there "for fear of the Jews" and had the doors bolted fast. Nothing suggests that they regarded Sunday as a holy day. Only eight texts in the New Testament mention the first day of the week, and none of them suggest that it is sacred.

Q: Well, if the Bible doesn't teach Sunday observance, where did the idea come from, anyway?

A: "And he shall . . . think to change times and laws" (Dan. 7:25). "Thus have ye made the commandment of God of none effect by your tradition" (Matt. 15:6). "In vain they do worship me, teaching for doctrines the commandments of men" (verse 9). "Saying, Thus saith the Lord God, when the Lord hath not spoken" (Eze. 22:28).

God predicted that such a thing would happen, and it did. Misguided individuals of long years past sought to tamper with God's holy law and claimed that His holy day had been changed from Sabbath to Sunday. Today most Christians unwittingly accept it as fact. Sunday observance is nothing more than a human tradition, one that violates God's law, which commands Sabbathkeeping. Only God can make a day holy. God blessed the Sabbath, and when God blesses, no human being can "reverse it" (Num. 23:20).

25. MARK OF THE BEAST [MB]

The mark of the beast involves accepting a human-made law contrary to God's Ten Commandments. One day soon human beings will have to make a final decision for or against the full Ten Commandments.

1—Dan. 7:23-25	4—Rev. 14:9-11	8—Rev. 14:4, 5
2—Rev. 13:16-18	5—Rev. 16:1, 2, 10, 11	9—Rev. 7:4
(cf. Ex. 13:9)	6—Ps. 37:23-25, 31-34	10—Rev. 14:1-3
3—Rev. 13:7, 8	7—Rev. 15:2	

ADDITIONAL NOTES

A time will come that God's Sabbath will act as a great test of obedience. All of earth's inhabitants will have to face its claims. At that point, when the issues stand clearly revealed, individuals will accept either the seal of God or the mark of the beast. The book of Revelation describes a final edict of earth's governments that will actually seek to enforce the mark upon all the world. "And he causeth all, both small and great, rich and poor, free and bond, to receive a mark in their right hand, or in their foreheads" (Rev. 13:16). It is evident that no one has the mark until human governments force the decision upon all humanity. Then the issues of the true Sabbath and the counterfeit Sunday will be so clear that no one can escape making a decision either to honor the true Sabbath with mind and hand or to submit to the counterfeit worship day of the antichrist.

Comments from those of various denominations:
"We have made the change from the seventh day to the first day, from Saturday to Sunday, on the authority of the only holy catholic, apostolic, church of Christ" (Bishop Seymour [Episcopal], *Why We Keep Sunday*).

"It is true there is no positive command for infant baptism. . . . Nor is there any for keeping holy the first day of the week" (Amos Binney [Methodist], *Theological Compend,* by Amos Binney, pp. 180, 181, Methodist.

"There was and is a commandment to 'keep holy the Sabbath day,' but that Sabbath day was not Sunday. . . . There is no scriptural evidence of the change of the Sabbath institution from the seventh to the first day of the week" (Edward T. Hiscox, *The Baptist Manual*).

Q: Which is the Sabbath day?

A: Saturday is the Sabbath day.

Q:. Why do we observe Sunday instead of Saturday?

A: We observe Sunday instead of Saturday because the Catholic Church transferred the solemnity from Saturday to Sunday.

Q: By what authority did the church substitute Sunday for Saturday?

A: The church substituted Sunday for Saturday by the plentitude of that divine power which Jesus Christ bestowed upon her" (*The Convert's Catechism of Catholic Doctrine,* p. 50).

26. TITHING [T]
We rob God when we don't return to Him 10 percent of our income and give offerings as we are able.

1—Deut. 8:18	6—1 Cor. 9:14	11—Deut. 14:22
2—1 Tim. 6:7	7—Num. 18:21	12—Lev. 27:30, 32
3—Luke 12:34	8—2 Cor. 9:7	13—Matt. 23:23
4—Ps. 24:1	9—Mal. 3:8-10	14—Heb. 7:5
5—Ps. 96:8	10—Gen. 28:22	

The tenth is certainly a small part of our material gain to render to God in recognition of His real ownership of all.

27. CHRISTIAN STANDARDS [CS]
A Christian's dress, words, and actions will reflect his or her inner spiritual experience.

1—James 4:4	8—Gen. 35:2, 4	15—1 Thess. 5:22, 23
2—1 John 2:15-17	9—Ex. 33:5	16—Ps. 101:3
3—Deut. 22:5	10—Ex. 35:22	17—2 Cor. 6:14-18
4—Jer. 4:30	11—1 Peter 3:3	18—Rom. 14:13
5—1 Tim. 2:9	12—Eze. 7:19	19—Ex. 32:1-4
6—Hosea 2:13	13—Isa. 33:15-17	20—Acts 7:38-43
7—Judges 8:24	14—Jer. 6:15	

ADDITIONAL NOTE

All Christians should dress modestly, healthfully, tastefully, and neatly, thus representing the principles of the heavenly kingdom.

28. TEMPLE OF GOD [TOG]
The physical body is the temple of the Holy Spirit, and we should care for it through what we eat and drink, or anything else that we do.

1—1 Peter 1:15, 16	10—1 Cor. 3:16, 17	19—Gen. 7:2
2—3 John 2	11—Prov. 23:2	20—Rev. 18:2
3—Isa. 55:2	12—2 Cor. 7:1	21—Gen. 1:29
4—Ex. 23:25	13—Lev. 20:25, 26	22—Gen. 2:16
5—Rom. 12:1	14—Lev. 11:26	23—Gen. 3:18
6—Deut. 34:7	15—Lev. 11:7	24—2 Cor. 6:17, 18
7—1 Cor. 6:10	16—Isa. 66:17	25—1 Cor. 10:31
8—Prov. 20:1	17—Lev. 3:17	26—Prov. 4:20, 22
9—1 Cor. 6:19, 20	18—Lev. 17:14	

29. HEALING THE SICK [HS]
God desires health and healing for all His followers.

1—Matt. 4:23	6—Luke 9:1, 2	11—1 Kings 13:6
2—Matt. 8:14-17	7—Acts 5:15, 16	12—Deut. 7:11, 15
3—Luke 8:48	8—Acts 28:8	13—2 Chron. 16:12
4—John 5:14	9—Ps. 103:2, 3	14—Mark 6:13
5—1 Cor. 12:28	10—James 5:14-16	

30. MARRIAGE [Mar]
Marriage is a beautiful, happy relationship between a man and a woman that God Himself established.

1—Gen. 2:24	7—Eph. 4:32	13—Eph. 4:26
2—Matt. 19:5, 6	8—Prov. 31:11, 12	14—Prov. 21:19
3—Rom. 7:2	9—Rom. 12:10	15—Ex. 20:17
4—Matt. 19:9	10—Col. 3:18, 19	16—Ps. 127:1
5—1 Peter 3:1	11—1 Peter 4:8	17—1 Cor. 7:10, 11, 13
6—1 Cor. 7:34	12—Prov. 15:1	18—Eph. 5:28-33

31. PREMARITAL SEX [PS]
When God created marriage to bless and make humanity happy, He established special guidelines to protect and preserve that special relationship.

1—1 Cor. 7:1, 2, 9	6—Eccl. 7:26	11—Gal. 5:19-21
2—Ex. 22:16	7—Mark 7:21-23	12—Eph. 5:3
3—Deut. 22:28, 29	8—Rom. 1:28-32	13—Col. 3:5, 6
4—Prov. 5:3-5	9—1 Cor. 6:9, 10	14—1 Thess. 4:3
5—Heb. 13:4	10—Jude 7	15—1 Cor. 6:18

32. SECOND COMING [SC]

Jesus announced a series of signs that would remind us of His soon-approaching return to earth. His followers need to keep in mind seven points about His second coming:
1. Countless angels will accompany the Lord. He will not come alone.
2. He will arrive in the clouds, and every eye shall see Him. The Second Advent will not be in secret.
3. The dead who have accepted Christ as their Savior will rise first in the resurrection.
4. The righteous living who are still alive at the Second Advent will be caught up with the resurrected dead to meet the Lord in the air.
5. The wicked living are destroyed.
6. The wicked dead will remain in their graves for 1,000 years.
7. The righteous will reign with Christ for 1,000 years.

1—Joel 2:31
2—2 Tim. 3:1-5
3—2 Peter 3:3, 4
4—Dan. 12:4
5—Matt. 24:3-7
6—Matt. 24:14

7—Rom. 1:29-31
8—Matt. 24:32-38
9—John 14:2, 3
10—Matt. 24:44
11—Matt. 25:31
12—Matt: 24:30, 31

13—1 Thess. 4:16, 17
14—Rev. 1:7
15—2 Thess. 2:8
16—Jer. 4:26
17—Titus 2:13
18—Heb. 9:28

33. DEATH [De]

When a person dies, he or she rests unconscious in the grave till Jesus comes.

1—Gen. 2:7
2—James 2:26
3—Job 27:3
4—Job 4:17
5—1 Tim. 6:16
6—Eccl. 9:10, 5, 6

7—Ps. 115:17
8—Acts 2:29, 34
9—1 Cor. 15:51, 52
10—1 Thess. 4:16, 17
11—Eze. 18:20
12—Gen. 3:4

13—Job 7:9, 10
14—John 11:11-14
15—Ps. 13:3
16—John 5:25-28

34. HELL [He]

After the 1,000 years following the second coming of Jesus, hell will exist on this earth. The wicked will burn until they turn to ashes and vanish forever, and hell itself will cease.

1—John 3:16
2—Matt. 16:27
3—Luke 12:47, 48
4—Job 21:30
5—John 5:28, 29
6—Matt. 13:40-42
7—Jude 1:7
8—2 Peter 2:6
9—Rev. 20:9
10—Rev. 21:8
11—Ps. 37:10
12—Mal. 4:1
13—Eze. 18:20
14—Rom. 6:23
15—Isa. 47:14
16—Ps. 37:20
17—Isa. 65:17
18—Matt. 10:28
19—Isa. 1:28
20—Eze. 33:11
21—Nahum 1:9
22—Rev. 21:1

35. 1,000-YEAR REIGN [TYR]

Christ's second coming will leave the earth desolate. The redeemed will examine heaven's records and confirm God's judgment of the wicked dead, who have already sealed their destiny by their rejection of Christ. Satan will find himself bound on this earth with no one to tempt during the millennium.

1—Rev. 20:1-3
2—Jer. 4:23-27
3—Rev. 20:4
4—1 Cor. 6:2, 3
5—Rev. 20:7, 8
6—Rev. 21:2
7—Rev. 20:9
8—Rev. 21:1, 27

36. SANCTITY OF LIFE [SL]

Sin devalues life, as we see so dramatically portrayed in the world today, but the Word of God emphasizes its preciousness in His sight.

1—Ps. 139:13-16
2—Ps. 127:3
3—Ex. 21:22-25
4—Luke 1:41, 44
5—Gal. 1:15, 16
6—Jer. 1:5
7—Gen. 9:6
8—Ex. 23:7
9—1 Peter 4:15
10—Micah 6:7, 8

37. JUDGMENT [J]

We will have to answer in God's judgment for everything that we say, do, or think. The only way to escape the consequences of wrong things is by confessing our sins and accepting Jesus Christ as Lord and Savior.

1—Eccl. 3:17	7—Rev. 14:6, 7	13—Eccl. 12:13
2—Acts 17:31	8—Rev. 20:12, 15	14—Heb. 7:25
3—Rom. 14:12	9—Ps. 56:8	15—Prov. 28:13
4—Eccl. 12:14	10—Mal. 3:16	16—1 John 2:1
5—Luke 8:17	11—Ps. 50:6	
6—Matt. 12:36, 37	12—James 2:10, 12	

38. HEAVEN AND NEW EARTH [HNE]

After 1,000 years in heaven God's people descend to the earth along with the New Jerusalem. The wicked are raised and, during their attack on the Holy City, perish in a rain of fire and brimstone. God then creates a beautiful new earth for the redeemed.

1—1 Cor. 13:12	6—Matt. 5:5	11—Mal. 4:2
2—Isa. 66:22, 23	7—Isa. 40:31	12—Isa. 35:1
3—Rev. 21:1-4	8—Isa. 35:5, 6	13—Isa. 65:21-25
4—1 Cor. 2:9	9—Gen. 3:22	14—Matt. 8:11
5—Ps. 16:11	10—Rev. 22:1, 2	

SUMMARY

As we near the end of time, Satan will so mingle falsehood with truth that only those who have the guidance of the Holy Spirit will be able to distinguish truth from error. We need to make every effort to follow the Lord's leading and teaching. Never should we turn from Him and put our trust in human beings. Every day we are to come to Jesus with full assurance of faith and to ask Him for wisdom. Those guided by the Word of the Lord will discern with certainty between falsehood and truth, between sin and righteousness.

LET'S REVIEW . . .

1. How much of the Bible can I believe (study 1, p. 9)?
2. How may I have salvation (study 3, p. 9)?
3. Who is the Creator of all things (study 5, p.10)?
4. What are the four kingdoms of Daniel 2 (study 6, p.10)?
5. What must take place in peoples' lives before they can enter heaven (study 9, p. 18)?
6. How does one communicate with God (study 13, p. 19)?
7. What are the identifying marks of God's people (study 14, p. 19)?
8. What should every baptized Christian be doing (study 16, p. 20)?
9. False churches will teach against what (study 17, p. 20)?
10. What does baptism symbolize? What takes place when we are baptized? (study 18, p. 20)?
11. Why should Christians practice the ordinance of foot washing (study 19, p. 21)?
12. What is one identifying mark of God's remnant church (study 20, p. 21)?
13. How are people saved, and are the Ten Commandments still important today (study 21, p. 21)?
14. What is the fourth commandment and should we obey it (study 22, p. 22)?
15. What is true Sabbathkeeping (study 23, p. 22)?
16. Does the Bible tell us to substitute Sunday for the Sabbath (study 24, p. 22)?
17. What is the mark of the beast (study 25, p. 25)?
18. How much of what I own belongs to God? What does God require each Christian to render to Him (study 26, p. 26)?
19. What kind of lifestyle should Christians live (study 27, p. 27)?
20. How does God regard the human body? What kinds of food should we avoid (study 28, p. 27)?
21. What does God think about marriage (study 30, p. 28)?
22. What seven events will take place at Jesus' second coming (study 32, p. 29)?
23. What happens when a person dies (study 33, p. 29)?
24. When does hell take place (study 34, p. 20)?
25. Where will the redeemed dwell during the 1,000 years (study 35, p. 30)?
26. What is our only way to live through the judgment (study 37, p. 31)?
27. What happens at the end of the 1,000 years (study 38, p. 31)?

You can give a Bible study!

Yes, *you*!

This little guide outlines an easy Bible marking system that chain-references texts for 38 different topics. Using only your Bible, you can share the life-changing answers to questions about important spiritual matters. Additional notes are included to help you explain difficult or complex subjects.

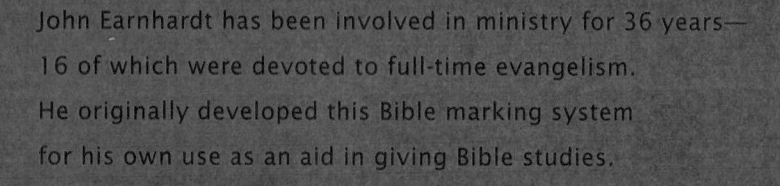

John Earnhardt has been involved in ministry for 36 years—16 of which were devoted to full-time evangelism. He originally developed this Bible marking system for his own use as an aid in giving Bible studies.

Bible Study

REVIEW AND HERALD®
PUBLISHING ASSOCIATION
Since 1861 | www.reviewandherald.com

ISBN 978-0-8280-2400-6